TOEFL WRITING

IMPORTANT TIPS & HIGH SCORING SAMPLE ANSWERS!

(Written By A TOEFL Teacher)

By Daniella Moyla

TOEFL Writing

Copyright 2015 by Daniella Moyla

Published by Sanbrook Publishing

All rights reserved. No Part of this book may be reproduced or transmitted in any form or by any means without the written permission of the author.

Limits of Liability / Disclaimer of Warranty:

The author and publisher of this book and the accompanying materials have used their best efforts in preparing this program. The author and publisher make no representation or warranties with respect to the accuracy, applicability, fitness, or completeness of the contents of this book. They disclaim any warranties (expressed or implied), merchantability, or fitness for any particular purpose. The author and publisher shall in no event be held liable for any loss or other damage, including but not limited to special, incidental, consequential, or other damages.

This manual contains material protected under International and Federal Copyright Laws and Treaties. Any unauthorized reprint or use of this material is prohibited.

TOEFL® iBT is a registered trademark of Educational Testing Service (ETS). The material in this text has been created completely by the author, Timothy Dickeson. This material is not endorsed or approved by ETS.

Table of Contents

Why You Should Read This Book 1
Task 1 - Integrated Writing 3
    What Is Task 1? 3
    Suggested Answer Structure 3
    Task 1 Question Types 4
    Key Things To Focus On To Prepare Your Answer 5
    What You Must Brainstorm Before Your Start Writing Your Answer 6
    Scoring Criteria 6
    High Scoring Task 1 Sample Answers 8
        Sample Answer – (Positive Relationship) 8
        Sample Answer – (Negative Relationship) 11
Task 2 - Independent Writing 14
    What Is Task 2? 14
    Suggested Answer Structure 14
    Task 2 Question Types 15
    What You Must Brainstorm Before Your Start Writing Your Answer 20
    Scoring Criteria 21
    TOEFL Writing Tips 21
    High Scoring Task 2 Sample Answers 23
        Sample Answer – (Agree or Disagree) 23
        Sample Answer – (Preference) 25
        Sample Answer – (If / Imaginary) 27
        Sample Answer – (Description / Explanation) 29
        Sample Answer – (Comparison and Contrast) 31
About the Author 33

Why You Should Read This Book

The TOEFL can be a very daunting exam to achieve a high score in. The significance of the TOEFL can be the difference between obtaining a visa or position at a university for many people. Therefore, it is important that if you require a specific TOEFL score, you review what makes high quality writing answers before you take the exam.

All too many people take the TOEFL several times without reaching their desired score and do not understand why.

This book has been written specifically for people like you who want to view sample writing answers that comply with the standards of TOEFL scoring criteria and would achieve a high score if written for a TOEFL exam.

Many sample answers on the internet today are not quality reviewed and can be misleading.

These answers however have been written by a professional TOEFL teacher with more than 10 years' experience who has used these methods to reach high scoring results with most of her students.

If you want to succeed on the TOEFL, then this book will assist you in understanding what is required.

You should read this book if:

- You have taken the TOEFL exam before and did not obtain a high score in the writing section and don't know why.

- You have searched the internet for sample answers but you are unsure of the quality of the answers and who wrote them.

- You have never taken the TOEFL exam and you want to review how high scoring answers are structured, so you can follow a similar format.

- Your TOEFL exam is very soon and you need last minute guidance on how to write high scoring answers.

Task 1 - Integrated Writing

What Is Task 1?

In Task 1 of the TOEFL writing section, you are given a reading passage and a listening passage. You are then required to write an answer and explain how the two passages relate to each other, whether they are contradicting or share the same view.

You will always be given the reading passage first and the listening passage and then the question which will ask how they relate to each other.

You are given 20 minutes to plan, write and revise your essay and it should be between 150-250 words long for an optimal score.

Suggested Answer Structure

You should structure your answer in four different paragraphs (although the fourth paragraph is optional and is only used if you have enough points to discuss):

1. **Introductory paragraph:** introduce the main idea of the answer and clearly state what the overall answer to the question is.

2. **First key point:** using a key point which is covered in both the reading and listening, discuss the relationships between the two passages.

3. **Second key point:** using a second key point which is covered in both the reading and listening, discuss the relationships between the two passages.

4. **Third key point (only if there is a third key point):** using a third key point which is covered in both the reading and listening, discuss the relationships between the two passages.

Task 1 Question Types

In task 1, there are really only two different question types. However, you will receive only one type when you take the TOEFL:

- **Positive relationship:** This type infers that the reading and listening passages have the same general opinions on the topic and the question will generally ask how the listening supports the reading.

- **Negative relationship:** This type infers that the reading and listening passages have different general opinions on the topic and the question will generally ask how the listening casts doubt/contradicts the reading.

Key Things To Focus On To Prepare Your Answer

One of the main things that help people achieve a high score for this task is by doing necessary preparation. This is done by taking appropriate notes and focussing on the things that matter from the reading and listening passages.

Below are the key things you MUST do during the reading and listening passages:

- **Take notes** – This will help you remember the things from the passages and help you to include details in your answer

- **Focus on identifying key points from both passages** – During the reading passage, you must focus on the key/important points that are being made. This is because these key points will also be discussed in the listening passage and it is relationship between the reading and listening on each point that you must include in your essay.

- **Identify the relationship (positive or negative)** – The relationship between the reading and listening will either be positive (both have the same opinion on the topic), or negative (have different opinions on the topic. You must identify this relationship before you start writing your essay because this will help you decide on the direction of your essay.

What You Must Brainstorm Before Your Start Writing Your Answer

When you receive the question, you must immediately brainstorm the following items:

1. What the direction of the relationships is between the reading and listening (positive or negative).

2. Summary sentences for the reading and listening (what each passage is about in general).

3. Key points from the reading passage (2 or 3 points).

4. Key points from the listening passage (2 or 3 points).

5. The relationship between the reading and listening for each key point.

Scoring Criteria

You will be assessed according to the following criteria:

- **Task Achievement:** how well and thoroughly you answer the question.

- **Comprehensibility:** how well the evaluator can understand your whole essay and the ideas you discuss throughout.

- **Organisation:** how well your essay is structured.

- **Flow of Ideas:** how well ideas/discussions flow together, and how well your paragraphs and sentences linked together.

- **Grammatical Range and Accuracy:** the variety of grammar structures you use and how well you use them.

- **Vocabulary:** the variety of vocabulary you use and how well you use them.

High Scoring Task 1 Sample Answers

Sample Answer – (Positive Relationship)

Reading Passage

"It is common knowledge that **forecasting** is an attempt by meteorologists to determine what weather will be like in the future. **Hindcasting** is the opposite of forecasting, an attempt to determine what weather was like in the past. Meteorologists wish that records of weather had been kept in full for at least a few millennia, but it has been only in the last century that detailed records of the weather have been kept. Thus, meteorologists need to hindcast the weather, and they do so by using all sorts of information from other fields as diverse as archeology, botany, geology, literature, and art. These pieces of information from other fields that are used as a basis for drawing conclusions about what the weather must have been like at some point in the past are called **proxies**."

Listening Passage

(Professor): "Now let me talk about how hindcasting was used in one particular situation. This situation has to do with the weather in seventeenth-century Holland. It appears, from proxies in paintings from the time by numerous artists, that the weather in Holland in the seventeenth century was much colder than it is today. Seventeenth-century paintings show really cold winter landscapes with huge snow drifts and ice skaters skating on frozen canals. Since it's unusual today for snow to drift as high as it is in the paintings and for the canals to freeze over so that skaters can skate across them as they are in the paintings, these paintings appear to serve as proxies that demonstrate that the weather when the paintings were created in the seventeenth century was much colder than it is today."

Question:

Summarize the points made in the lecture, being sure to specifically explain how they strengthen specific points made in the reading passage.

Answer:

In this set of materials, reading passage discusses a technique used by meteorologists, and in the listening passage, the lecturer talks about one specific example of hindcasting. He states that this method provides a good example to demonstrate how the weather was in the seventeenth century in Holland.

From the reading passage, it is outlined that proxies in paintings illustrate that the weather in Holland in the 17 century was significantly colder that today. These paintings indicate very cold environments and also show people skating on frozen canals. The listening passage also clarifies that these proxies help to provide information about weather in the past simply by using paintings as proxies

Secondly, it is very unusual today for snow to drift as show in the paintings. In the listening passage, the professor talks about an example where hindcasting was used. The example is where paintings were used as proxies to show that Holland was colder in the 17th century than today. In many of the 17 century paintings, it can be seen that the weather was much frigid than today. For example, there were skaters who were skating on canals but these canals are not frozen today. In addition, there were snow drifts that were much higher than the snow drifts that are experienced today.

In summary, the reading passage demonstrates the effectiveness of the hindcasting method to make assumptions about historical weather. The listening passage further discusses and supports this method by providing a key example of how hindcasting is used.

Word count = 252

Sample Answer – (Negative Relationship)

Reading Passage

In a vote that took place at the International Astronomical Union Conference on August 24th, 2006, Pluto lost its status as a planet in our solar system. Pluto was originally discovered in 1930 when scientists were searching for something that was interfering with Uranus's orbit. Though Pluto was estimated to be similar in size to Earth, it was later discovered that it was even smaller than our own moon, as well as many other moons. It is now known that there are thousands of planetary objects similar to Pluto, including Eris which is slightly larger than Pluto. Choosing to reclassify Pluto to a dwarf planet honors the fact that science is about making new discoveries. While it was a sad day for Pluto lovers, people in general have accepted the idea, and the next generation of children will grow up knowing only eight planets and thinking nothing of it. As Mike Brown, the astronomer who discovered Eris, noted following the IUC's decision, "science is self-correcting.

Listening Passage

(Professor): "As you all likely know by now, Pluto has been officially demoted to a dwarf planet. What this means is that we will no longer include it as part of our solar system. The debate about whether or not Pluto should hold its status as a planet created such a conflict within the community of world astronomers that it has been called the Great Pluto War. The decision on whether or not to demote Pluto was put to a final vote by astronomers from around the world at the International Astronomical Union Conference. However, when I say from around the world, I don't mean worldwide. In fact, less than 10% of the world's astronomers voted, and most of those who were at the conference had already gone home by the last day when the vote took place. Of more than 10 000 potential voters, less than 500 took part, mainly because there was no way for them to cast their vote without actually being at the conference. Many astronomers believe that if electronic voting had been an option, Pluto along with two other celestial objects, would now be considered planets. Furthermore, the definition that was decided upon for a planet - that it must clear the neighborhood around its orbit - doesn't technically hold up, since Earth, Mars, Neptune, and Jupiter all have asteroids as neighbors.

Question:

> Summarize the points made in the lecture, explaining how they cast doubt on the points made in the reading passage.

Answer:

From the material provided, the reading text discusses the decision to remove Pluto as a planet in our solar system and the listening part explains that this decision may not have been comprehensive and nor correct. The professor covers two key points which demonstrate that the listening part casts doubt on the main ideas of the reading text.

Firstly, the professor states that only 10% of the world's astronomers actually voted. There were potentially over 10,000 people that could have voted, however les that 500 concluded that Pluto should be removed from our solar system. The low number of voters was due to voting constraints, where they needed to be physically at International Astronomical Union Conference.

Secondly, the listening passage also outlines that the definition of a planet is not consistent because not all planets fit the technical criteria. The decided definition of a planet states that it must clear the neighborhood around its orbit. However, Earth is an example where it has asteroids as neighbors, which also illustrates that the decision to make Pluto a dwarf planet has been a conflict within the astronomical field.

In summary, the reading passage implies that science is an ever-changing field and that decisions are constantly made based on new information which means the decision about Pluto is correct. However, in contrast, the professor outlines key points which demonstrate that this decision is not one that is agreed by many astronomers.

Word count = 239

Task 2 - Independent Writing

What Is Task 2?

In Task 2 of the TOEFL writing section, you are requested to write an opinion-based essay regarding a perspective, argument or problem.

You are given 30 minutes to plan, write and revise your essay and you need to write at least 250 words.

Suggested Answer Structure

You should structure your answer in at least four different paragraphs:

1. **Introduction:** This paragraph should present the topic of the question as well as the writer's position or guideline of what the essay will discuss.

2. **Body Paragraph 1:** This paragraph should describe the first point/reason or view in discussion. A successful paragraph consists of a Topic Sentence, explanation and examples.

3. **Body Paragraph 2:** This paragraph should describe the second point/reason or view in discussion. The structure should be the same as body paragraph 1.

4. **Conclusion:** This paragraph should restate the writer's position and also summarize the main points discussed in the essay.

Task 2 Question Types

In task 2, there are five possible question types. You will receive one these in the TOEFL exam.

AGREE OR DISAGREE

This question type usually proposes an extreme argument and you are requested to either agree or disagree with it.

There are two similar cases in the Agree or Disagree question type:

Case 1) Agree or disagree. In this case, you are asked to take a position regarding the statement in the question. You can either completely agree/disagree or partially agree.

Example:

> "The only way to reduce the increasing crime rates is to apply stricter laws and tougher punishments to offenders. **Do you agree or disagree** with this statement?"

Case 2) To what extent do you agree or disagree. This case is identical to the previous one, the only difference is the way the question is worded. Therefore, you are asked to take a position regarding the statement in the question. You can either completely agree/disagree or partially agree.

Example:

> "Given the increasing rates of obesity worldwide, it should be compulsory for all children to practice at least one sport at school. **To what extent do you agree or disagree?**"

PREFERENCE

This question type usually presents two points of view of the same issue and asks you to then give your preference with reasons why your prefer that option.

Two opposite views. You are given two different preferences on a particular topic and you are asked which option you would prefer. You will always be required to provide specific reasons and examples to support your preference. Two important aspects of this question are that both positions need to be mentioned, and your must use very clear and specific reasons to support your preference.

Example:

> "**Some people prefer** to work as an employee. **Others prefer** to start a business. **What would you prefer?** Use specific reasons and details to support your answer."

IF / IMAGINARY

This question type usually gives a conditional question and asks you what you would do in a particular (hypothetical) situation using specific reasons and examples to support your opinion.

Conditional question. You are given a hypothetical question using the word 'would' which means you must answer the question also using the conditional structure. This means that it is important to be familiar with using the word 'would' (2nd conditional) because you are describing something that is not real at this point in time.

Example:

"What change **would** make to your local park to benefit the local community? Use specific reasons and examples to support your opinion."

DESCRIPTION / EXPLANATION

This question type usually presents and type of person or place and asks you to describe or explain the characteristics or qualities of that person or place.

Illustrate. You must provide specific characteristics and expand on why these characterises relate to the person or place given in the question. This means that it is important to identify reasons that directly to the person or place using specific examples and justification.

Example:

"Police Officers are very important in keeping people safe. In your opinion, what are the **qualities** of a good Police Officer? Use specific details and examples in your answer."

COMPARISON AND CONTRAST

This question type usually provides a statement about a topic with a requirement to compare and/or contrast or provide the advantages and/or disadvantages of a specific method or opinion of the statement.

There are two similar cases in the Comparison and Contrast question type:

Case 1) Compare and Contrast. In this case, you are asked to discuss the two sides of a topic focusing on both the similarities and the differences. It is important to discuss both, not just the similarities or differences.

Example:

> "It has been quoted, "You can't learn everything from a book." **Compare and contrast** knowledge obtained from practical experience with knowledge obtained from books. In your opinion, which is better? Why?"

Case 2) Advantages and Disadvantages. In this case, you are asked to discuss the pros and cons of something. Alternatively, you may be asked to describe only the advantages of two systems or even outweigh the advantages and disadvantages of an idea. Similar to the previous case, the most important aspect of this question is that both perspectives need to be discussed. Taking just one stand is not an option.

Example:

"Modern food preparation and packaging technologies have allowed the creation of ready-to-eat meals. These have become extremely popular and supermarket aisles have been filled with this type of foods. What are the **advantages and disadvantages** of consuming these foods? Provide your opinion and five specific reasons for your choice."

What You Must Brainstorm Before Your Start Writing Your Answer

When you receive the question, you must immediately identify and brainstorm the following items:

1. What the question type is (this will help you determine how you will structure your essay)

2. What the parts are to the question, and what your direct answers are for each part (this will help you formulate your introduction and also make sure you answer all of the questions).

3. Key reason/discussion point for the second paragraph (also brainstorm example(s) to use to help support your reason/discussion point).

4. Key reason/discussion point for the third paragraph (also brainstorm example(s) to use to help support your reason/discussion point).

Scoring Criteria

You will be assessed according to the following criteria:

- **Task Achievement:** how well and thoroughly you answer the question.

- **Comprehensibility:** how well the evaluator can understand your whole essay and the ideas you discuss throughout.

- **Organisation:** how well your essay is structured.

- **Flow of Ideas:** how well ideas/discussions flow together, and how well your paragraphs and sentences linked together.

- **Grammatical Range and Accuracy:** the variety of grammar structures you use and how well you use them.

- **Vocabulary:** the variety of vocabulary you use and how well you use them.

TOEFL Writing Tips

- Organize your response well using the appropriate structure

- Make sure your essay has clear sections

- Use transition words to guide your reader in a logical, organized way

- Leave enough time to proofread and check your essay, by checking spelling, punctuation and grammar errors

- Make sure your examples support your ideas (Task 2)

High Scoring Task 2 Sample Answers

Sample Answer – (Agree or Disagree)

Question:

> In these current times, living in big cities has become expensive, dangerous and stressful. It offers no benefits. To what extent do you agree or disagree?

Answer:

Life in big cities has always been a popular trend. Migration from small towns to big urban areas has increased throughout the years in most countries. Nonetheless, some people claim that city life has become more of a hassle than a solution. I tend to agree with this statement, however I believe it is a personal choice and several factors need to be considered.

To start with, it is easy to agree with this view for several reasons. First of all, buying houses in big cities has become almost unaffordable for families. This has forced many people to rent for many years or to buy a house in the outer suburbs far form city centres. Moreover, it is fair to say that there are higher crime rates in metropolitan areas such as car theft, burglaries and more violent crimes. Finally, the fact that most big cities tend to have a higher density of population, more traffic jams, crowded systems of transportation, and long commuting time, can make life in the metropolis quite hectic.

On the other hand, it is untruthful to suggest that big cities offer no advantages. This is because metropolitan areas offer a variety of resources and facilities that would be very problematic to access in smaller towns. One of the main reasons people migrate to the big cities is to educate themselves. The reason for this is that rural areas usually do not have quality educational institutions, especially for tertiary education. The same could be said in regards to health facilities and jobs. The best hospitals and biggest companies are generally located in urban areas.

Overall, it is difficult to take a position with such a relevant topic. But it is my view, that even though living in big cities can be challenging for different reasons, it also provides opportunities that can't be overlooked.

Word count = 307

Sample Answer – (Preference)

Question:

Some people prefer to work as an employee. Others prefer to start a business. What would you prefer? Use specific reasons and details to support your answer.

Answer:

Throughout history, there has always been two key ways to earn a living, by working as an employee and starting a business. Even though working as an employee has many benefits, for me starting a business is more ideal due to the flexibility it gives me and the amount of income I can earn from a business.

To begin with, I would prefer starting a business because I can choose the hours I work, which gives me more flexibility for my lifestyle. I am lucky enough to have a beautiful wife and young son, however looking after my son keeps me very busy. Although running a business can be hectic, I can choose the hours I want to work which gives me more freedom to be with my son, where as being an employee would be more restrictive in this case.

Secondly, working as an employee generally means that you have the same salary every week, fortnight or month. This can be good for some people but it also means that if you work harder, you still earn the same amount. As an example, my uncle works for a construction company and he works very long hours but he always earns the same amount each month regardless if he works on the weekend or not. If I start a business, the amount of money I earn depends on how hard I work. I could potentially earn a lot more running a business than working as an employee which makes starting a business also more attractive for me.

In conclusion, working as an employee can be a fantastic choice and suits many people around the world. However, starting business provides far more benefits for me than working as an employee.

Word count = 289

Sample Answer – (If / Imaginary)

Question:

What change would make to your local park to benefit the local community? Use specific reasons and examples to support your opinion.

Answer:

Parks are fantastic places because they provide open spaces within built up cosmopolitan areas. However, does this mean that all parks necessarily benefit the community? If I had the opportunity to change something about my local park, I would build a playground. There are two key reasons why I would make this change.

Firstly, playgrounds provide an attractive place for children to play which gets them outside and exercising. These days too many children spend a lot of time indoors watching TV or on the computer. Providing a playground would incentivise children to want to go outside and play which makes them healthier from the exercise they do. As an example, my son loves going to any playground. This makes me happy to see him outside and exercising as opposed to being inside.

In addition, building a playground would also provide a bonding place for parents and children. Often, parents are very busy either working or doing housework and this sometimes means that they are unable to spend quality time with their children. Quality bonding time has been proven to be very important to a child's upbringing. To illustrate, when I take my son to the playground we always have a lot of fun because I am not distracted by anything else and I know my son appreciates me playing with him. Having a playground at my local park would certainly assist in allowing parents to bond more with their children.

In summary, the first thing I would change to my local park to benefit the community would be to have a playground built because it would support healthy living in several different ways.

Word count = 274

Sample Answer – (Description / Explanation)

Question:

> Police Officers are very important in keeping people safe. In your opinion, what are the qualities of a good Police Officer? Use specific details and examples in your answer.

Answer:

Police officers are a vital part in maintain a safe community for everyone. Even though police officers are everyday people, there are several qualities which make a good police officer. Being fair when dealing with potential criminals and maintain strong physical strength are two key qualities that a police officer should have.

To begin with, when dealing with potential criminals, it can be very difficult to manage situations where they are being very aggressive and, or argumentative in defending their actions. Police officers sometimes need to make difficult decisions about whether or not to charge a person, which mean they must be fair when dealing with all types of people so the right decisions can be made. They need to listen to all sides to the story in order to identify exactly what happened. For example, I recently witnessed a car crash which was caused by two different drivers. When the police, they listened to both drivers to determine what happened, which showed that being fair to both drivers allowed the police to understand exactly what happened without jumping to a quick conclusion.

Secondly, strength is a very important quality because of the situations that police officers are commonly in. When dealing with aggressive people, it is important that police officers are able to physically control them in order to protect incident people nearby. This means that being physically strong helps police officers to manage these types of people. My brother in law is a police officer and he has told me many times that it he was not big and strong he would find dealing with aggressive people very difficult and it would also put him in danger.

Overall, being a police officer is a very noble profession and not everybody is capable of working in this job. However, being fair and maintaining a strong body are two key qualities which make good police officers.

Word count = 316

Sample Answer – (Comparison and Contrast)

Question:

It has been quoted, "You can't learn everything from a book." Compare and contrast knowledge obtained from practical experience with knowledge obtained from books. In your opinion, which is better? Why?

Answer:

It has been said that most of the world's knowledge is held in books. Books provide information on just about any topic you desire which means anyone can learn just about anything from a book. However, there is debate as to the effectiveness of learning from books whereby some people believe you can't learn everything from a book.

Some people believe that learning from practical experience is much more beneficial that learning from books. Experience on one hand can provide people with a much more visual approach to learning, where if you can see what you need to learn and start practicing to can learn the skill much faster than from a book. As an example, driving a car is a skill that can only be taught from practical experience. It would be very difficult to read a book about driving and then start driving immediately.

Driving takes time and requires hours behind the wheel to become used to different situations.

On the other hand, reading a book allows people to very quickly learn skills that may be difficult to learn from practical experience. Books can be found from a library or the Internet virtually immediately which means anyone can learn a topic of their choice very quickly. For example, it would be very difficult for me to learn about the country of Denmark from practical experience without going there. However, reading a book on Denmark could give me a lot of information all about the country very quickly, and also a lot cheaper.

Even though practical experience does provide the ability to learn difficult skills, I believe the ability read a book one anything I want is much better. I like the fact I can decide to learn about wood work by simply finding a book on the internet and downloading it is less than 5 minutes. I also like the fact that I can choose what chapters I want to read first based on what I want to know.

Word count = 331

About the Author

Daniella Moyla

Daniella is a highly sought after TOEFL consultant due to her ability to make TOEFL easy for people to understand.

Daniella is a degree qualified English teacher with expertise in ESL, academic English, TOEFL and TOEFL preparation.

Born in Chile, English is not her first language which has allowed her to understand the difficulties faced by anyone taking the TOEFL exam.

Daniella has written several TOEFL training courses which demonstrates her comprehensive understand of the TOEFL and the requirements for achieving a high score.

Her love of teaching also inspires her to continue following her passion of helping as many people as possible pass the TOEFL.

Printed in Great Britain
by Amazon